Circle of Fifths for Guitar

The Ultimate Guide for Guitarists:
Learn and Apply Music Theory,
Master Chord Progressions
and Become a Better Musician

by James Shipway

Circle of Fifths for Guitar
by James Shipway

Published by Headstock Books
headstockbooks.com

Copyright © James Shipway 2021

All rights reserved. This book or parts thereof may not be reproduced in any form, stored in any retrieval system, or transmitted in any form by any means - electronic, mechanical, photocopy, recording, or otherwise - without prior written permission of the publisher, except as provided by the United Kingdom copyright law. For permission requests, contact: info@headstockbooks.com

Book Cover Design by ebooklaunch.com

Paperback ISBN: 978-1-914453-60-1
Hardcover ISBN: 978-1-914453-62-5 / 978-1-914453-63-2
Ebook ISBN: 978-1-914453-61-8

Search for 'james shipway guitar' on YouTube and
subscribe for hours of free video lessons!

Join my online community at **totalguitarlab.com** and
get instant access to *all* my premium guitar courses *plus* live training,
workshops and Q&A sessions.

Contents

Introduction 1
Part 1: Circle of Fifths Basics 3
    Lesson 1: Introducing the Circle of Fifths 3
    Lesson 2: Going Round the Circle 8
    Lesson 3: Learning the Circle of Fifths 11
Part 2: Circle of Fifths Secrets 15
    Secret 1: Learn Your Guitar Neck with One Easy 'Grip' 15
    Secret 2: Use the Circle of Fifths as a Powerful Practice Tool 20
    Secret 3: Major Scale Tricks 24
    Secret 4: Easily Find the Chords in Any Key 32
    Secret 5: The Relative Minor Trick 37
    Secret 6: I, IV and V Chord Tricks 42
    Secret 7: Finding II-V-I Chord Sequences 48
    Secret 8: Finding I-VI-II-V Chord Progressions 52
    Secret 9: Finding III-VI-II-V-I Chord Progressions 55
    Secret 10: The 'Visual Formula' for Circle of Fifth Chord Progressions 57
Final Words 61
Free Video Masterclass 63
Appendix 1 64
Appendix 2 64
Appendix 3 66
Appendix 4 67
Appendix 5 68
The Circle of Fifths 71
Useful Resources 72

Introduction

Welcome to the *Circle of Fifths for Guitar*!

I still remember when a gifted teacher at music college introduced us to the circle of fifths.

To say it was mind blowing is an understatement!

Suddenly almost everything I knew about music took on a whole new dimension. I could see *why* things worked, *why* they sounded good, and being able to spot many of the 'formulas' which make up so much of the music we hear made learning and remembering new songs *so* much easier.

I wrote this book in the hope of giving you those same 'aha' moments that lesson gave me, so that *you* too can learn to use the amazing power of the circle of fifths!

How To Get Awesome Results with This Book

This book can do wonderful things for your playing and musicianship ...*if* you use it the right way.

I'd suggest following these guidelines:

1. **Go through the lessons in order**

This way, the easier concepts covered first will help you get familiar with using the circle of fifths before you tackle the more complex ideas later

2. **Don't be in a rush!**

It's not about reaching the end of this book, it's about what you discover along the way. Go through each lesson slowly and at your own pace so that you can absorb everything I show you

3. **Make it practical**

This doesn't have to be one of those 'dry' theory books which you'll quickly lose interest in. Use it as a **practical guide** for learning how to *apply* the circle of fifths to your instrument. Throughout the book I'll be encouraging you to play as many of the examples as you can on your guitar so that you can hear what they sound like. Doing this will help you retain the knowledge and gain a much deeper understanding of each concept. For some examples I give you chord shapes to use. These are optional, feel free to use *different* chord shapes to the ones shown if you prefer

4. Read my first Theory for Guitarists book!

I'm assuming you understand the theory basics taught in '**No Bull Music Theory for Guitarists**'. I'm referring to the first in the series of my three books on guitar theory. In this book, I'll be using terms like '**I-IV-V**', 'relative minor' and others, without explaining them in great detail. So, make sure you've got the basics down, and anything you don't understand, refer back to it in my first theory book.

5. Do the Quick Quiz questions

To help you check your understanding, I'll be testing you with some '**Quick Quiz**' questions along the way. Work through every quiz and check your answers alongside those I give you. It's the best way to make sure you understand everything

6. Download your Circle of Fifths BONUS pack!

Don't forget to download the extra resources which come with this book. They include a circle of fifths **wall chart** to stick up in your practice space as well as a **45 minute video masterclass** showing you some of what we're going to cover. These will really help you out, so go to the following webpage and grab your bonus pack now!

jamesshipwayguitar.com/circle

That's about it for now, I think we're ready to jump in.

I'm really excited about what you're going to learn from this book, so good luck and let's get started!

Part 1: Circle of Fifths Basics

Lesson 1: Introducing the Circle of Fifths

Before we look at all the cool things we can do with the circle of fifths, there are some basic things you need to know.

What is the Circle of Fifths?

You've probably seen the circle of fifths represented as a circular diagram like you see here:

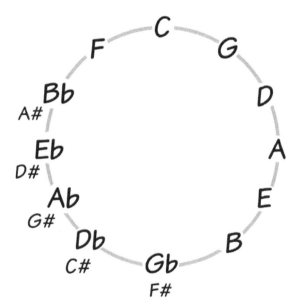

It's basically all 12 musical notes set out in a certain order and arranged in a circle. In the diagram the notes down the left-hand side of the circle are shown with both their sharp and flat name. Most of the time in this book we will only see the flat names in the circle. This is just because it makes it a little simpler to read (more on this in a moment).

If you're thinking:

This circle of fifths thing looks like some kind of weird scientific nuclear equation …I'm outta here!

Then wait! The circle of fifths *can* look a bit intimidating at first, but don't be put off!

Once we begin to break it down, you'll see how simple it really is. Just stick with these lessons, and soon everything will make perfect sense.

Important Note!

I just want to make something clear before we jump in. Sometimes you will see the circle of fifths written out 'backwards' compared to how I'm showing it to you in this book. The notes are still in the same order, they just go in the *opposite* direction. Sometimes, this version of the circle of fifths is called the *circle of fourths*.

Which method a musician uses really depends on individual preference, but when *most* people think of the circle of fifths, they think of it laid out as it in this book. This is the reason why I've chosen to use this format of the circle of fifths in these lessons.

Don't let all this confuse you, simply follow the instructions I give you in this book and you'll be fine. Just be prepared to sometimes see other books or teachers use a slightly different approach to what I'm showing you.

Cycle or Circle?

Sometimes you might hear someone talk about the *cycle* of fifths.

This is simply an alternative name for the *exact same thing*.

So, whether it's *circle* of fifths, or *cycle* of fifths doesn't matter. They are the same.

What Do We Use the Circle of Fifths For?

You know those 'multi-tools' you can get for fixing your bike?

They contain all the different sized wrenches, allen keys, screwdrivers and other tools you might need, all folded up into one compact and easy to use tool, literally a toolkit in your pocket.

The circle of fifths is a bit like this!

When we know how to use it then it becomes a powerful musical tool for any musician.

We can use the circle of fifths to:

Find the chords to use in any key

Figure out the chords for a 12 bar blues in any key

Move songs and chord sequences quickly and easily into other keys

Figure out the notes in a particular scale

And much more!

We'll be looking at how to do all of these things and more very soon, but in case you're wondering whether the circle of fifths will help you, the answer is almost definitely yes!

Why Are the Notes in this Order?

In my opinion, understanding *why* the notes are in the order that they are is actually not that important.

Some teachers may disagree with me about this, but I think it's more important to know *how to use* the circle of fifths than it is to know *why* it's laid out the way it is.

So, if you don't instantly understand the following explanation for the order of the notes, don't be put off, it won't stop you from doing all sorts of cool things.

With that said, let's look at the logic behind the order of the notes.

Hopefully you're familiar with the concept of 'intervals'? This is the system we use in music to describe and explain the distance between two notes.

If you know nothing about intervals, then what I'm about to say may be a little confusing, but don't worry, you just need to do a bit of catching up. Check out chapter 5 of **No Bull Music Theory for Guitarists** for a straightforward explanation of intervals.

Going **clockwise** around the circle the notes are arranged in intervals of a **5th**, also known as a ***perfect 5th***.

If we start on C, the next note in the circle is G, the perfect 5th interval of C.

The next note is D, the perfect 5th of G.

And so on, all the way around the circle of fifths.

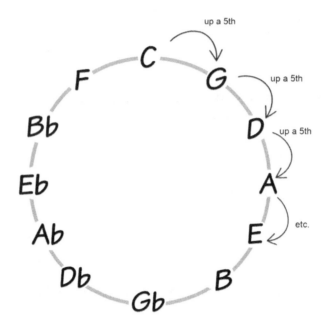

So remember, each time we go to the next note in a **clockwise** direction we are going up the interval of a **perfect 5th**.

If we go the other way, in an **anticlockwise** direction, the notes go up in **4ths** or **perfect 4ths**.

So, starting on C, the next note in the circle going anticlockwise is F, the perfect 4th interval of C.

The next note is B♭, the perfect 4th of F. This pattern carries on all around the circle:

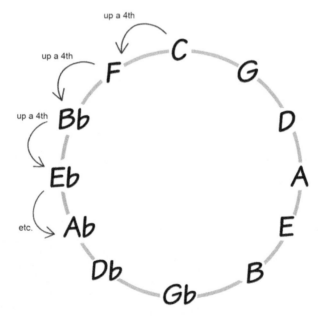

This is why the circle of fifths is sometimes called the circle of fourths, depending on which direction we go, we move in 4ths or 5ths.

Flats and Sharps

Let's go back to the topic of sharp and flat names as touched on a moment ago.

Hopefully you know that all flat (*b*) and sharp (#) notes have two names.

For example:

B*b* is also called **A#**
E*b* is also called **D#**
A*b* is also called **G#**
D*b* is also called **C#**
G*b* is also called **F#**

If you're not familiar with this concept then see *Chapter 1: The Musical Alphabet* in my **No Bull Music Theory for Guitarists** book.

To keep things simpler, we are going to use the **flat name** for these notes *most* of the time in this book. Occasionally I will use the sharp name instead.

Please don't think that I've left the sharp notes out of the circle. Using one name for these notes instead of both names just makes things easier in the early stages of learning to use the circle of fifths.

Just be aware of *both* names when it comes to the flat notes, and as you work through these lessons, you'll start to get an idea of which one is the correct name to use in a particular situation.

That's it for this first lesson, you now have a basic understanding of the circle of fifths.

Before you move on, do this **Quick Quiz** to test your knowledge. Check your answers and make sure you re-read the sections on any questions you get wrong before heading to Lesson 2!

Quick Quiz

1. How many notes are in the circle of fifths?
2. Are the notes arranged in a random order?
3. What is another name used for the circle of fifths?
4. Is the order of the notes exactly the same no matter which name is used?
5. Going in a *clockwise* direction, do the notes move in 4ths or 5ths?
6. Going in an *anticlockwise* motion do the notes move in 4ths or 5ths?
7. Any flat (*b*) notes in the circle can also be described as what?

Answers: **1.** There are 12 notes in the circle of fifths: the 12 notes in the 'musical alphabet' or chromatic scale **2.** No, the order of the notes is *not* random **3.** Another common name for the circle of fifths is the *cycle* of fifths **4.** Yes, no matter which name is used, the order of the notes remains the same **5.** Going clockwise the notes go up in 5ths **6.** Going anticlockwise the notes go up in 4ths **7.** Any flats can also be called by their sharp (#) name.

Lesson 2: Going Round the Circle

Welcome back!

We are going to be moving around the circle of fifths in both directions and it's crucial that you understand which way I am telling you to go in my instructions.

If I tell you to move **forward** around the circle, I'm telling you to travel in a **clockwise** direction as shown in this next diagram:

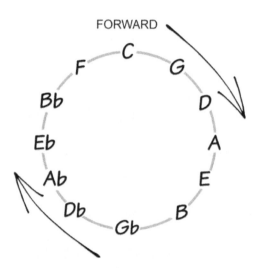

If I tell you to go **back** then I mean to go in an **anticlockwise** direction:

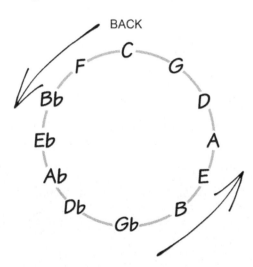

If you don't grasp this, then things are going to get mighty confusing for you, so just to make sure, here it is again:

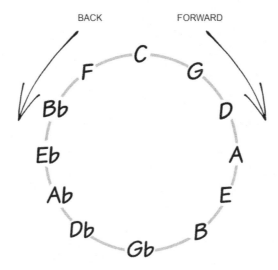

I'll also be talking about taking **steps** around the circle. One 'step' is like going to the next note in the circle. Thinking of each note as a 'step', is my way of describing how far to move forward or back around the circle of fifths.

Let's look at some quick examples. If we started on C and went **forward 1 step** we would go to the next note in the circle: G. If we went **forward 3 steps**, we would land on A.

We won't always be starting on C. The system works just the same whichever note we begin on. For example, if we started on E♭ and went **forward 2 steps** we'd land on F.

You can see these three examples in the following diagram:

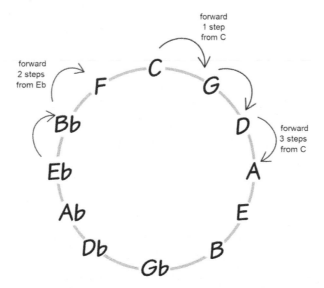

Going back works in just the same way. When we start on C and go **back 1 step** we land on F.

Start on A♭ and go **back 5 steps** and we land on A.

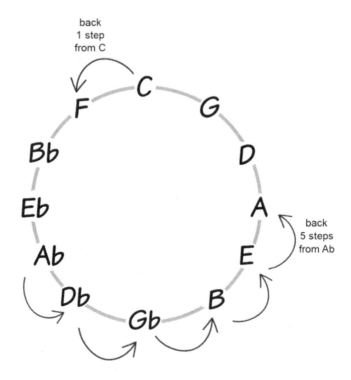

You might be wondering why any of this matters?

It's because I'll be giving you instructions or *formulas* for working things out using the circle of fifths. These will be explained in terms of going forwards or backwards a specific number of steps. If you go in the wrong direction or take the wrong number of steps, then these formulas won't work!

I'm not saying that this is the *only* way to explain how to use the circle of fifths, but this is the way that worked for me when I was taught it, and it's worked well for hundreds of my guitar students.

It'll work for you too, so we'll stick with it for now.

Read through the last few pages again and check that you are 100% happy with everything covered. It's essential if you're going to get anything at all out of this book! Then, answer the **Quick Quiz** that follows.

Check your answers against those given and make sure to re-read anything you don't quite understand.

When you're done, I'll see you in the next lesson.

Quick Quiz

Use the circle of fifths to answer the questions given.

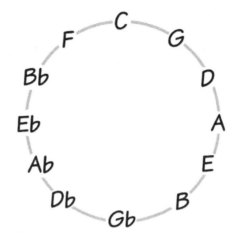

1. Start on C and go **forward 2 steps**. Which note do you end up on?
2. Start on C and go **forward 6 steps**. Which note do you end up on?
3. Start on C and go **back 2 steps**. Which note do you end up on?
4. Start on C and go **back 4 steps**. Which note do you end up on?
5. Start on A and go **back 2 steps**. Which note do you end up on?
6. Start on A and go **forward 3 steps**. Which note do you end up on?
7. Start on B*b* and go **back 2 steps**. Which note do you end up on?
8. Start on B*b* and go **forward 1 step**. Which note do you end up on?

Answers: **1.** D **2.** G*b* **3.** B*b* **4.** A*b* **5.** G **6.** G*b* **7.** A*b* **8.** F

Lesson 3: Learning the Circle of Fifths

Looking at the circle of fifths diagram every time you need to will get you so far.

But if you want to *really* master the awesome power of the circle of fifths, then you need to learn it from memory!

Luckily, I've got two simple 4 minute exercises to get the circle of fifths *engraved* into your mind in no time.

First, we're going to learn the order of notes going in a **clockwise** direction (that's forward ...right?).

Exercise 1

Let's begin with the notes down the right hand side of the circle of fifths.

1. Grab your phone and set a countdown timer for 1 minute
2. Press start on the clock
3. Read and say the following note names slowly, looking at each one as you say it:

C G D A E B G♭

4. When the clock stops, rest for about 30 seconds
5. Now once more, start the clock and repeat the note names slowly, looking at each one as you say it
6. When the clock stops, rest for 30 seconds
7. Start the clock again and repeat the note names slowly, looking at each one as you say it

There's nothing revolutionary about this exercise, but having a short step-by-step method gives us a quick and efficient way to memorise something. It also makes us more likely to take action!

Now, let's do the same with the remaining notes.

Exercise 2

1. Set a countdown timer for 1 minute
2. Press start on the clock
3. Read and say the following note names slowly, looking at each one as you say it:

G♭ D♭ A♭ E♭ B♭ F C

4. When the clock stops, rest for about 30 seconds
5. Now once more, restart the clock and repeat the note names slowly, looking at each one as you say it
6. When the clock stops, rest for 30 seconds
7. Start the clock again and repeat the note names slowly, looking at each one as you say it

If you've just completed these exercises then great. If not, stop right here and do them now, they're really important!

So, how do these exercises relate to the circle of fifths?

When we start on C and go forward until we reach G♭, we get the first set of notes you learned.

When we go forward from *Gb* and return to C, we get the second set of notes.

All we did was split the sequence of notes in the circle into two sets to make them easier to learn.

Look at the last circle of fifths diagram and see this for yourself.

Your Tasks for this Lesson

There's no **Quick Quiz** for this lesson!

Instead, do **Exercise 1** and **Exercise 2** every day for a week.

This will take less than an hour in total and trust me, it's well worth the effort!

After doing these exercises, test yourself by going around the following diagram naming the note which belongs in each box:

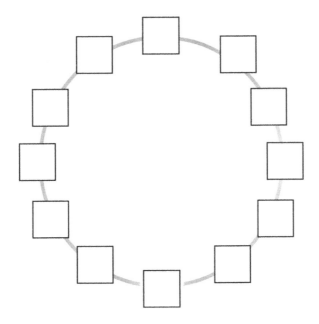

After a few days you'll be able to recite the notes as they appear in the circle and you'll have a good idea of what it looks like visually. Both of these factors are important.

If you want to become a true circle of fifths *master*, then I suggest you also memorise the notes in **reverse** order. In other words, start on C, and learn to recite the notes going *backwards* around the circle. This will be a huge help to you as you work through these lessons.

Many readers won't bother with this, but I highly recommend that **you** do!

Ready for some circle of fifths 'secrets'?

Congratulations on completing Part 1 of *Circle of Fifths for Guitar*!

If you understand everything covered so far and have successfully learned the circle of fifths, then you're ready for the circle of fifths 'secrets' coming next.

So, without further ado, let's look at 10 incredibly useful things we can do with the circle of fifths.

See you in Part 2!

Part 2: Circle of Fifths Secrets

Secret 1: Learn Your Guitar Neck with One Easy 'Grip'

Many guitar players never bother to learn the notes on the guitar fingerboard.

Here are some of the reasons why:

1. It's not the most interesting or fun thing to do on the guitar!
2. They don't know how to do it
3. They know they *should* do it, but just never get around to it
4. You can play the guitar without knowing them (to some extent anyway)

Eventually, this gap in their knowledge becomes a problem.

Let me be clear: **not** knowing the notes on the guitar can seriously hold up your guitar playing!

I'm guessing that if you're interested in the circle of fifths then you're a serious and committed guitarist, and this means you *need* to know the notes on the guitar fretboard.

If you don't know them already, then now is a great time to stop and learn them, you see, knowing the notes in the circle of fifths makes this job easy!

The Circle of Fifths 'Grip'

Grab your guitar and play this shape anywhere on the neck:

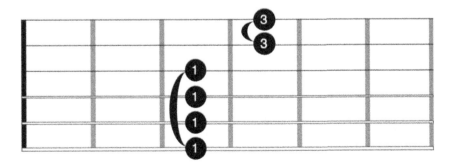

Believe it or not, this is actually a chord shape (just probably not one you've seen before).

It's also a *killer* way to learn *all* the notes across the guitar strings.

Here's how it works:

1. Play the shape at any fret on the guitar. We'll start on C up at the 8th fret

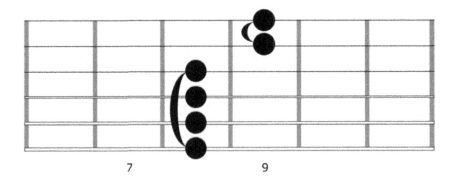

2. Starting on C go **back 5 steps** in the circle of fifths saying the notes as you go:

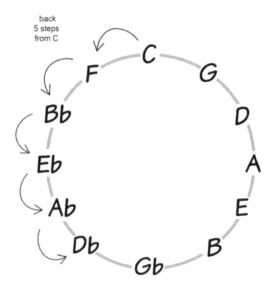

This gives us: **C**, **F**, **B*b***, **E*b***, **A*b***, **D*b***

Now look at the notes in the grip. They're labelled in the following diagram.

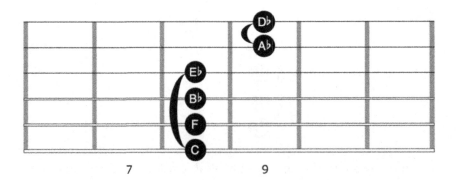

They're the exact same notes!

This works anywhere on the guitar, simply:

1. Play the shape at any fret
2. Determine the note you are starting the shape from on the low E string
3. Beginning on that note, go **back 5 steps** in the circle of fifths (*now* do you see why I suggested learning the circle of fifths in reverse order as well?)
4. And you get the notes going across the strings

How cool is that?

Obviously, you need to know the notes along the low E string to use this method, but I'm guessing you probably already do, we use them all the time to move common scales and barre chord shapes around. If you don't yet know the notes along the low E string, start learning them using **Appendix 1** found in the back section of this book to help.

Let's look at one more example before you try some on your own. This time we'll start on G:

1. Play the shape at the 3rd fret:

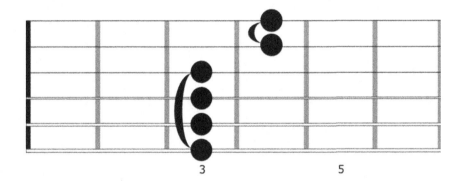

2. Starting on G, go **back 5 steps** in the circle of fifths saying the notes as you go:

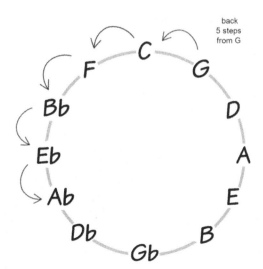

This gives us: **G, C, F, B**b**, E**b**, A**b

As before, these are the notes found on the strings as you work your way across the grip:

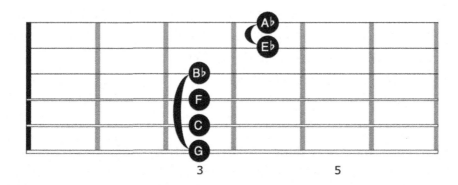

Now, Test Yourself!

Apply the 'grip' method to find the notes at the following frets:

1. Starting on E (12th fret)
2. Starting on B*b* (6th fret)
3. Starting on A (5th fret)

Here's what you should have got:

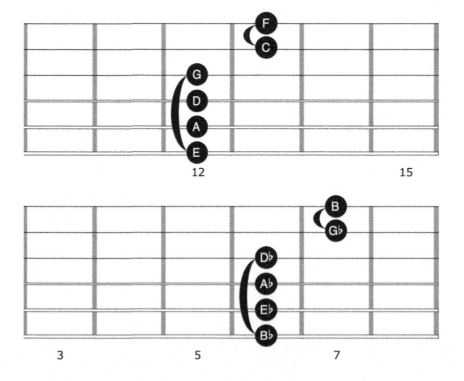

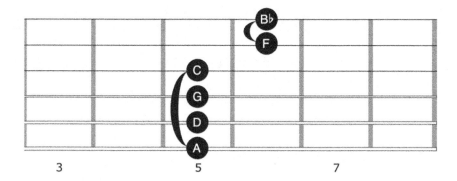

Eventually you'll know the notes on your fretboard so well, that you won't need to use the grip to work them out, but this method sure makes it easier to get started.

Before we leave this lesson, here is the grip applied to *all* the natural notes along the E string.

Of course, this method works starting on flat and sharp notes as well, I've just left them out to make the diagram less cluttered and easier to use.

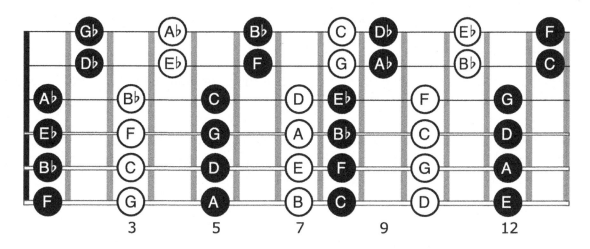

And that's your first circle of fifths 'secret'. Spend some time getting familiar with this and use it to start memorising all the notes on your fingerboard. You don't need to do them *all* at once, work slowly and methodically up the neck until you've covered every fret.

Knowing the notes will help you move chords and scales around more easily, play in different keys, write songs, improvise more freely and lots more, so jump in and start using the circle of fifths 'grip' to master them all!

Good luck, have fun, and I'll see you in the next lesson when you're ready.

Secret 2: Use the Circle of Fifths as a Powerful Practice Tool

The circle of fifths is an amazing practice tool and many *legendary* musicians have used it to help develop their skills.

In this lesson I'll show you a few ways that you can use it when you practice too.

Why is the circle of fifths such an awesome practice tool?

To become a great musician, we need to bash through the limitations and obstacles which can hold us up. One of the best things we can do in order to achieve this, is to make sure we can play tools like scales and chord shapes starting on any note.

For example, you may be confident using a barre chord shape to play a G chord, but can you use that same shape to play a D*b* or F chord just as easily?

And can you move that familiar A blues scale shape up the neck so that you can use it to jam over a 12 bar blues in D or E*b*?

And, even if you know how to do these things in theory, can you do them quickly and easily, or do you need to stop and work it all out?

I think you get the idea, the more fluently you can move things around the guitar neck the better your guitar playing is going to become.

The circle of fifths contains all 12 musical notes, making it a great way to sharpen up these skills. If we can play a scale or chord starting on each note in the circle, then we *know* we can use it in lots of different settings and keys. The versatility this gives us is game changing!

Let's look at three powerful circle of fifths practice exercises.

Exercise 1: Nailing Barre Chords with the Circle of Fifths

You're probably familiar with this common 'E shape' major barre chord with the root on the low E string:

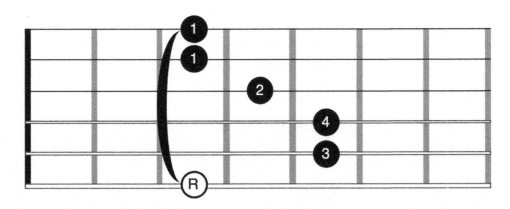

This chord shape can be used to play any major chord, just use the root note on the E string to work out where on the neck to play it. If we move the shape so that the note on the low E becomes D, then we are playing a D chord.

Move the shape so the low E note becomes F, and we get an F chord.

I'll assume you know all this, but if you don't, then check out my **No Bull Barre Chords for Guitar** book and audio set. It's available on Amazon, Apple, Google Play, Kobo, Barnes & Noble and other platforms. You can also ask your local bookshop or library to order it for you.

Now, assuming you know how barre chords work, how fluent are you at using them to play *any* chord?

Let's find out.

Try the following **practical exercise**:

1. Start at the top of the circle. Using the barre chord shape from earlier, play a C chord
2. Go **forward to the next step**: G. Move the barre chord shape to play a G chord
3. Go to the **next step** and play a D chord
4. Work your way around the circle, playing the chord shape starting on each note you come to

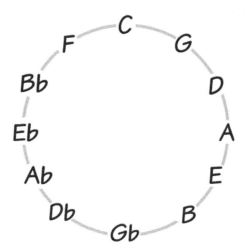

Imagine how, with a bit of practice on this exercise, you could sharpen up your barre chord skills!

Instead of hunting around trying to work it out 'on the fly', you'll know *exactly* where to move a shape to get *any* chord you need.

This means you can focus on playing the music, instead of struggling to work out where to move your chord shapes to.

Of course, we can also adapt this exercise to master *any* other chord shapes we want to.

This simple but powerful exercise is a great addition to your practice routine. Give it a go, it really works.

Exercise 2: Jam in Any Key with the Circle of Fifths

Imagine being able to play a solo in any key, on the spot!

The circle of fifths can help you learn to do this, here's how.

Normally we use a scale shape when we play a solo, for example, over a 12 bar blues in the key of G we'd probably use the G minor pentatonic or G blues scale.

Just like barre chords, most scale shapes can be moved around the neck into other keys too.

You guessed it: you're going to move a scale shape around the circle of fifths.

Let's use this common minor pentatonic pattern as an example. Here it is in the key of C:

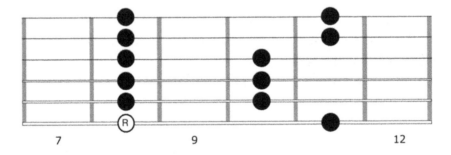

You probably already know that this shape can be used to play *any* minor pentatonic scale. Just like with the barre chord shape, we use the root on the E string (the first note in this pattern) to work out where to play it on the fretboard to get the specific scale we need.

Move the shape to the 10th fret and the root note becomes D, giving you D minor pentatonic, perfect for jamming over a blues in D or in the key of D minor.

Move the shape so that the root note becomes F at the 1st fret and we get an F minor pentatonic scale, and so on.

Practicing playing the scale around the circle of fifths will help you rapidly learn to move it around the guitar neck so that you can use it to solo in any key without difficulty.

Now try this **practical exercise**:

1. Start at the top of the circle. Using the scale pattern, play a C minor pentatonic scale
2. Go **forward 1 step** to G. Play a G minor pentatonic scale
3. Go **forward 1 step** to D. Play a D minor pentatonic scale
4. Work your way around the entire circle of fifths starting the scale on each note

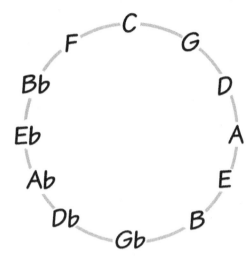

Congratulations, you just played all 12 minor pentatonic scales using the same scale shape.

With a bit of practice, you'll instantly know where to move the scale to for whichever key you need to solo in (no more embarrassing jam session scenarios).

We've chosen a really common scale pattern for this demonstration, but this works for almost *any* other scale too. Try it with some other scales you know and see for yourself what a powerful exercise this is.

Exercise 3: Circle of Fifths Feedback!

I don't mean the kind of feedback you get when you turn your amp up loud!

I'm talking about the feedback we get from *doing* the two exercises I just gave you. For example, you may find that you can easily move the scale or barre chord into C, E or G, but when you get to A*b* or D*b* your mind goes totally blank!

This kind of feedback is good: it shows us where we need to improve, and the circle of fifths is *brutal* at exposing these weak areas in our playing.

We need to listen to this feedback, learning from the exercise, then we need to respond to it. Here's how:

1. On a piece of paper, draw a *new* circle diagram containing *only* the keys you have problems with written in a random order.

   For example, imagine I was weak at moving the barre chord shape around to play B*b*, D*b*, B and F. I would use only these notes in my new circle, written out in any order I liked.

It might look something like this:

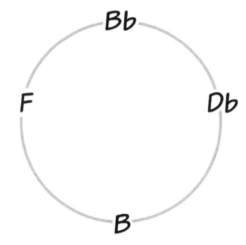

2. Next, I'd play the chord shape clockwise around this new circle. By doing this I'm focusing only on my weaker areas and improving them

3. When it felt easier, I'd go back to the original exercise and play around the entire circle of fifths to see if the problem areas have improved

This almost always fixes these kinds of problems, so remember this little trick.

Listening to the feedback from these or any exercises helps us to improve faster because we can easily spot and overcome the roadblocks that are holding us up.

So, use these exercises to fine tune your fretboard knowledge. Something, somewhere is holding you up, and using the circle of fifths could be the best way to spot it and methodically overcome it.

Of course, these are just a few of the ways you can use the circle of fifths in the practice room. There are many other applications, see if you can invent some to help with any specific problems you have.

So, grab your guitar and get going. I'll see you in the next lesson!

Secret 3: Major Scale Tricks

If you're reading this book then you will almost certainly have heard of the major scale.

It's no exaggeration to say that the major scale is the basis of most of the music you will probably ever hear. The notes in the major scale are like the 'raw material' we shape and craft into songs and melodies.

Now, you might be thinking:

But I hardly ever use the major scale! I use pentatonic and blues scales, and they work fine for me.

This is true for lots of guitar players, in fact, we can make amazing music on guitar without *ever* playing a major scale.

Knowing about the major scale is still *essential* knowledge for any guitar player though, enabling us to understand chord progressions, chord structure, intervals, keys, modes …and that's just for starters!

I'll assume you know the basics about the major scale already, but if you feel like there may be gaps in your major scale knowledge, then check out chapter 3 in my **No Bull Music Theory for Guitarists** book. This will teach you everything you need to know.

But now it's time for a few simple major scale 'tricks' using the circle of fifths. These will help you fine tune your knowledge of this crucial musical tool.

Let's dive in!

Find the Notes in Any Major Scale!

Knowing the notes in all of the 12 major scales is *incredibly* beneficial, but memorising them can be intimidating, it seems like something which is going to take a *long* time.

Luckily for us, knowing the circle of fifths makes this task much easier.

Here is the simple formula for working out the notes that make up *any* major scale:

1. Start on the **root** (starting note) for whichever major scale you want
2. Now skip **forward 5 steps**
3. Now go **back 6 steps**
4. That's it!

As you take the **6 steps back**, you land on each of the 7 notes in your major scale.

Cool shortcut, huh?

This is much easier to see visually, so let's apply it to the key of C with some diagrams.

1. Start on C and skip **forward 5 steps.** This puts us on B
2. Starting on B, now go **back 6 steps**

26 | CIRCLE OF FIFTHS FOR GUITAR

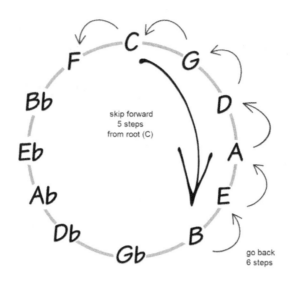

We land on **B, E, A, D, G, C** and **F**

These are the 7 notes in the C major scale.

If we arrange them alphabetically starting on the root (C) we get:

C D E F G A B

Make sense?

Let's use the same method to work out the notes in the B♭ major scale.

1. Start on B♭ and go **forward 5 steps**
2. Now go **back 6 steps**

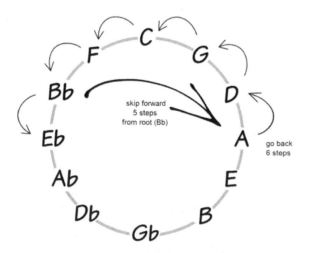

This gives us the notes:

A D G C F B♭ E♭

Simply arrange them alphabetically starting on the root and we get the B♭ major scale:

B♭ C D E♭ F G A

This trick works for figuring out the notes in *any* major scale, and makes learning all those note names seem *much* more manageable.

Sharp and Flat Names

I'm sure you're familiar with the idea that a 'flat' note can also be referred to as a 'sharp', for example, G♭ is also called F#.

If you do need clarification on this idea, then see chapter 1 of **No Bull Music Theory for Guitarists** for more information.

So far in this book, we have been leaving the sharp (#) notes out of the circle of fifths.

The problem is, that in some major scales, we want to describe the flat notes by their equivalent sharp name.

So, when do we need to do this?

All you need to do is remember this simple rule:

The notes down the *right* hand side of the circle of fifths all have sharps in their major scales, *not* flats.

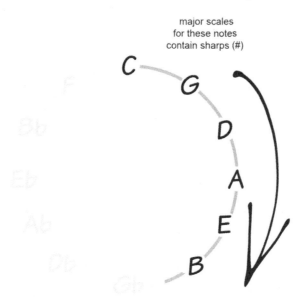

So, when we work out the notes in the major scales for **G**, **D**, **A**, **E** and **B** we need to convert any flat notes into their sharp equivalent.

For example, we **don't** call the notes in the A major scale:

A B D♭ D E G♭ A♭

The correct way to describe them is:

A B C# D E F# G#

We wouldn't call the notes in the B major scale:

B D♭ E♭ E G♭ A♭ B♭

The correct way to describe them is:

B C# D# E F# G# A#

Even though the notes are exactly the *same* thing, labelling them in this way is how it's done.

So, that's how you can use the circle of fifths to work out the notes in all 12 major scales, just remember that for the G, D, A, E and B major scales you need to convert any flats you get into sharps.

Before we continue, use the circle of fifths to work out the notes in the following major scales. Use the correct sharp or flat name where applicable!

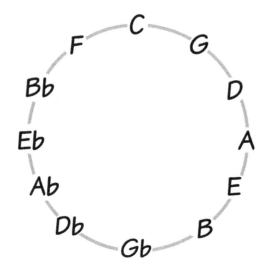

Quick Quiz

1. What are the notes in the F major scale?
2. What are the notes in the G major scale?
3. What are the notes in the E♭ major scale?
4. What are the notes in the D major scale?
5. What are the notes in the G♭ major scale?
6. What are the notes in the E major scale?

Answers: 1. F, G, A, Bb, C, D, E **2.** G, A, B, C, D, E, F# **3.** Eb, F, G, Ab, Bb, C, D **4.** D, E, F#, G, A, B, C#
5. Gb, Ab, Bb, Cb*, Db, Eb, F **6.** E, F#, G#, A, B, C#, D#

(***NOTE:** In *very* rare cases you may see B called *Cb* or E called *Fb*. Don't worry too much about this, it's not something you'll encounter that often)

Another Handy Major Scale Trick

Here's a great way to remember how many sharps or flats are in each major scale.

You'll remember that the notes in the C major scale are **C D E F G A** and **B**.

The C major scale is the *only* major scale which does not contain *any* sharp or flat notes. All the other major scales contain at *least* one sharp or flat.

Let's begin on C at the top of the circle of fifths.

If we go **forward 1 step** we land on G. The G major scale contains **1 sharp** (F#).

If we go **forward another step** we land on D. The D major scale contains **2 sharps** (F# and C#).

Go **forward another step** and we land on A. The A major scale contains **3 sharps** (F#, C#, G#).

Do you see a pattern emerging?

Every time we go **forward one more step**, we add *one more sharp note* than the previous major scale had.

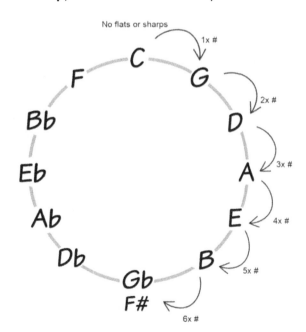

Here are the notes in the major scales for C, G, D, A, E, B and F# (shown as G♭ in the circle). You can see that each scale in the sequence has one more sharp note than the previous scale. Notice also how each time you add another sharp to a major scale, any sharps in the previous major scales remain.

C major: C D E F G A B
G major: G A B C D E **F#**
D major: D E **F#** G A B **C#**
A major: A B **C#** D E **F#** **G#**
E major: E **F# G#** A B **C# D#**
B major: B **C# D#** E **F# G# A#**
F# major: **F# G# A#** B **C# D# E#** (shown as G♭ in circle of fifths)

The exact same thing works for the major scales which contain flats. The difference is that this time we go back (anticlockwise) around the circle of fifths.

As before, begin on C at the top of the circle of fifths.

Go **back (clockwise) 1 step** and we land on F. The F major scale contains **1 flat** (B♭).

Go **back another step** and we land on B♭. The B♭ major scale contains **2 flats** (B♭ and E♭).

Going **back another step**, we land on E♭. The E♭ major scale features **3 flats** (B♭, E♭, A♭).

Again, a pattern emerges!

Each time we go **back one more step**, we add *one more flat note* than the previous major scale had. As with the sharps, any flat notes in the previous major scales remain.

C major: C D E F G A B
F major: F G A **B*b*** C D E
B*b* major: **B*b*** C D **E*b*** F G A
E*b* major: **E*b*** F G **A*b* B*b*** C D
A*b* major: **A*b* B*b*** C **D*b* E*b*** F G
D*b* major: **D*b* E*b*** F **G*b* A*b* B*b*** C
G*b* major: **G*b* A*b* B*b* C*b* D*b* E*b*** F

This trick isn't necessarily one you'll use a lot, but it's good to be aware of. It can help you understand the major scale more fully.

That's all on the major scale for now.

You'll just have to trust me when I tell you how useful knowing about the major scale is!

The deeper your understanding, the easier it is to:

1. Work out and remember songs
2. Compose your own chord sequences
3. Improvise riffs and solos over songs and chord sequences
4. Understand most of the important music theory you need to know

...and do a whole load of other things as well.

You can now use the circle of fifths to get really familiar with lots of helpful major scale theory. I know we haven't looked at actually playing major scales, it's not what this book is really about. If you do wish to play a major scale but don't know how, then see the useful scales shown in **Appendix 4** at the back of this book.

That's it for this lesson. Test yourself with the questions coming next and I'll see you again soon.

Quick Quiz

Starting on C, use the circle of fifths to work out how many sharps or flats are in the following major scales:

1. F
2. A
3. A*b*
4. D
5. G
6. B*b*
7. E*b*
8. B

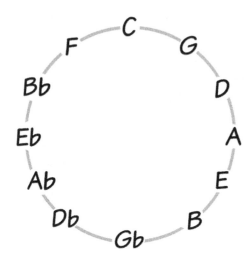

Answers: **1.** 1 flat **2.** 3 sharps **3.** 4 flats **4.** 2 sharps **5.** 1 sharp **6.** 2 flats **7.** 3 flats **8.** 5 sharps

Secret 4: Easily Find the Chords in Any Key

When you're writing a song in a certain key, how do you know which chords to use?

This next circle of fifths 'trick' can help!

You see, every key has a unique **chord family** made up of 7 chords. Broadly speaking, these chords will all work together and 'sound good' when combined into chord sequences. Understanding this can really take the mystery out of writing a good song.

If you're not familiar with the concept of keys and chord families then see chapter 7 in **No Bull Music Theory for Guitarists**. This breaks the idea down and makes it easy to grasp.

In this lesson I'll show you how to use the circle of fifths to easily work out all the chords in any major key chord family, a really handy thing to know.

Let's get into it!

Chord Roots

You're hopefully familiar with the idea of the 'root note'. This is the note a particular chord or scale is built on.

For example, the root of a C chord is C, the root of an Fm chord is F, and so on.

In any major key chord family, the roots of the chords are the 7 notes in the 'parent' major scale

So, the 7 notes in the C major scale will form the root notes for the 7 *chords* in the C major chord family. The notes in the E major scale are the root notes of the chords in the E major chord family, and so on.

So, the first thing to do when working out the chords in a chord family is to work out the notes in the parent major scale for that key. This is one reason why knowing the notes in the major scales is so incredibly useful, it allows you to easily work with chords and chord sequences.

A quick reminder of how to work out major scale notes using the circle of fifths:

1. Start on the **root** for the relevant major scale
2. Now skip **forward 5 steps**
3. Now go **back 6 steps** to get each of the notes in the scale

<u>**What Are the Chords?**</u>

Once we know the root notes for the chords, we need to determine the *quality* of each one. A chord's *quality* describes the type of chord it is; major, minor, diminished or whatever.

Say this little word sequence with me:

DIMINISHED, MINOR, MINOR, MINOR, MAJOR, MAJOR, MAJOR

This tells us the types of chord we get on each note in the major scale when we put the notes in the order that they appear in the circle of fifths.

Important: This only works when we put the notes in the order that they go around the circle of fifths! It doesn't work when we arrange them in *alphabetical* order (which we'll be doing in a moment).

If we start on C, skip **forward 5 steps**, then go **back 6 steps** we get the notes in the C major scale in the following order:

B E A D G C F

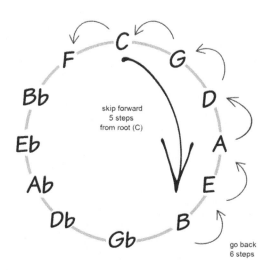

We can now use the word sequence as a handy way to work out what the chords will be:

DIMINISHED, MINOR, MINOR, MINOR, MAJOR, MAJOR, MAJOR

Applying it to the notes in the C major scale gives:

B Diminished, E minor, A minor, D minor, G major, C major, F major

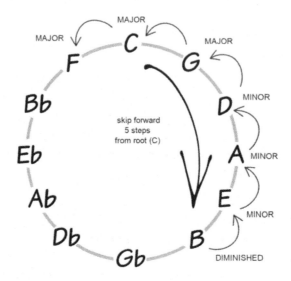

Remember, this trick only works when the notes in the major scale are arranged in the order in which they go around the circle of fifths.

When we arrange the chords alphabetically, they are still the same 7 chords, just in a different order:

I	II	III	IV	V	VI	VII
C	Dm	Em	F	G	Am	Bdim

It's also possible to arrange the notes alphabetically straight away and work out the chords using the common major, minor, minor, major, major, minor, diminished formula. See **No Bull Music Theory for Guitarists** for more on this.

Let's apply this idea to the key of B♭.

Using the formula we've looked at, work out the notes in the B♭ major scale.

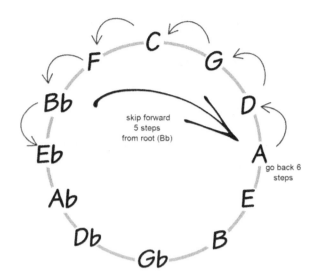

You should have this:

A D G C F B*b* E*b*

Apply the word sequence to tell you the quality of the chords, and you get:

A Diminished, D minor, G minor, C minor, F major, B*b* major, E*b* major

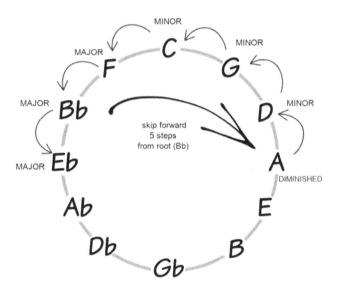

Now arrange them in alphabetical order starting on B*b*:

I	II	III	IV	V	VI	VII
B*b*	Cm	Dm	E*b*	F	Gm	Adim

See how it works?

So, to summarise:

1. Work out the notes in the relevant major scale
2. Apply the word sequence to determine the quality of each chord
3. Arrange them alphabetically
4. And you've got your chord family!

Although this process is fairly straight-forward, there are a few steps to it, so consider re-reading this lesson to check you understand everything.

When you're ready, use this method to work out the chords in the keys shown in the following table. Remember to check your answers to make sure you're on the right track with this.

When you're done, I'll see you in the next lesson!

Quick Quiz

Fill in the chords in the chord families shown. The C major chord family has already been done for you.

I (key)	II	III	IV	V	VI	VII
C	Dm	Em	F	G	Am	Bdim
A						
Eb						
F						
E						

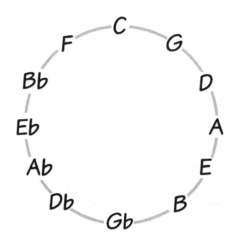

Let's do a **practical exercise** as well. Choose a chord family and using any chord shapes you know create some short chord progressions. Don't worry about the diminished (dim) chord for now, just use chords **I-VI**.

Answers:

I (key)	II	III	IV	V	VI	VII
C	Dm	Em	F	G	Am	Bdim
A	Bm	C#m	D	E	F#m	G#dim
Eb	Fm	Gm	Ab	Bb	Cm	Ddim
F	Gm	Am	Bb	C	Dm	Edim
E	F#m	G#m	A	B	C#m	D#dim

Secret 5: The Relative Minor Trick

Welcome back!

In this lesson I'm going to show you how to easily work out the **relative minor key** for any major key.

As we'll see, this is a handy thing to be able to do for *lots* of reasons.

I'm going to assume you already know what a relative minor key is. If you don't then it's not a problem, you'll find it explained clearly in *No Bull Music Theory for Guitarists*. Refer to that and then return to this lesson when you're ready.

Finding the Relative Minor

Working out the relative minor key is easy using the circle of fifths:

Simply go forward 3 steps from the major key, and you'll land on the relative minor key

For example, to find the relative minor key of C major:

1. Start on C in the circle of fifths
2. Now, go **forward 3 steps**

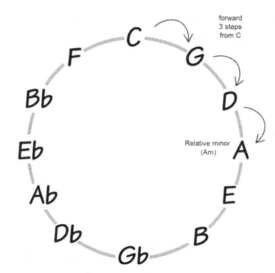

When you do this, you land on A, making the relative minor key A minor. The relative minor can also be thought of as chord VI in any major key chord family. Look at the table in the previous section (Secret 4), showing the C major chord family, and you'll see that in the key of C, the VI chord is A minor.

The sound of the I chord going to the relative minor is very common, and we'll be seeing it in some chord progressions later on. For a **practical exercise**, play C to Am using any chord shapes you know. *Listen closely to the way it sounds, this will help you learn to recognise this common chord movement by ear.*

Let's do another key.

To find the relative minor of D major, go **forward 3 steps** from D:

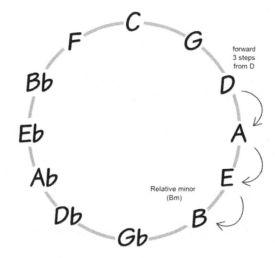

As you can see, the relative minor of D major is the key of B minor.

Easy right?

As a **practical exercise**, play D to Bm on your guitar to hear the sound.

Try the questions that follow to make sure you've got this concept. Use one of the circle of fifth diagrams in this book to help.

Quick Quiz

1. What is the relative minor of G major?
2. What is the relative minor of E major?
3. What is the relative minor of F major?
4. What is the relative minor of B*b* major?
5. What is the relative minor of A major?

Answers: **1.** Em **2.** C#m **3.** Dm **4.** Gm **5.** F#m

Using the Relative Minor

There are a few reasons why knowing the relative minor key is helpful, let's look at a few of them.

The Chords in the Chord Families are the Same!

As we've already seen, each major key comes with its own unique chord family which we use for playing chord progressions and music in that particular key.

Minor keys also have their own family of 7 chords. We use these for playing songs and chord progressions in a *minor key*.

Note: for more detailed lessons on chord families and minor keys see chapters 7, 8, 11 and 12 in *No Bull Music Theory for Guitarists*.

The cool thing is this: the chord families for any major key, and its relative minor key, are *exactly* the same!

Let's look at a quick example, here is the C major chord family:

I	II	III	IV	V	VI	VII
C	Dm	Em	F	G	Am	Bdim

The relative minor of C major is A minor. Study the A minor chord family shown in the following table:

I	II	III	IV	V	VI	VII
Am	Bdim	C	Dm	Em	F	G

You can see that the chords in the two families are the same, all we've done is make A minor the *first* chord in the minor key family.

This means that by knowing your major key chord families, you can easily work out the minor key chord families too.

Try this **practical exercise**:

1. Take the C major chord family and create a short chord sequence starting on the C chord
2. Now take the A minor chord family. Starting on the A minor chord, create some short chord sequences in the key of A minor

Hopefully you can hear how, even though the chords are the same, beginning on Am emphasises this chord, making the chord sequences sound quite different. Experiment with this idea for a while.

Minor Pentatonic Soloing in Major Keys

Most guitar players are familiar with the minor pentatonic scale and use it all the time to play solos and licks.

But sometimes we need to solo in a *major* key and for that we need to use the *major pentatonic* scale.

You might think this means that you can't use all your favourite minor pentatonic licks and ideas when you are soloing in a major key …

…but you can!

To solo in a major key, simply play the *minor pentatonic* starting on the *relative* minor.

For example, if you need to solo in C major, use any A minor pentatonic scale you know. Chances are, many of your favourite licks and minor pentatonic ideas will still sound good.

This trick works because the notes in C major pentatonic and A minor pentatonic are *exactly* the same.

This 'rule' applies to any major key and its relative minor key.

As another example, you could solo in the key of G major using E minor pentatonic scales. This is because E minor is the relative minor of G.

Make sense?

This handy trick can get you out of all sorts of scrapes if you're not familiar with using major scales or major pentatonics yet.

As a **practical exercise**, dig out some major key backing tracks to jam over. Use the circle of fifths to work out the relative minor key and practice jamming over it using minor pentatonic scales as described in this lesson.

So far, you know how to use the circle of fifths to learn notes on the guitar, as a practice tool, and for working out major scales, major keys and the relative minor.

This is just the beginning!

When you're ready, I'll see you in the next lesson where we're going to use the circle of fifths to learn to play the most common chord progression *ever*, in any key.

When you think you understand everything in this lesson, test yourself with the quiz coming next. Then when you're ready, I'll see you in the next lesson!

Quick Quiz

Using the circle of fifths, work out the relative minor key for each of the following major keys.

Try to use the correct name for any sharp or flat minor keys:

1. A
2. F
3. D
4. Ab
5. Eb
6. G
7. E
8. B

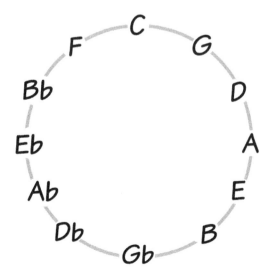

Answers: 1. F#m **2.** Dm **3.** Bm **4.** Fm **5.** Cm **6.** Em **7.** C#m **8.** G#m

Secret 6: I, IV and V Chord Tricks

There is one chord progression which is used extensively in *nearly all* music, whether it's rock, blues, country, pop, folk, or something else:

The I-IV-V chord sequence

The **I-IV-V** or 'one-four-five' chord progression is literally *everywhere* and the circle of fifths can help us master it.

So, in this chapter, we'll look at some useful circle of fifths tricks you can use to learn more about **I-IV-V** progressions.

What is I-IV-V?

I cover the **I-IV-V** sequence in more detail in chapter 9 of **No Bull Music Theory for Guitarists**, but here's a quick reminder.

The term 'one-four-five' refers to the three chords in a chord family labelled with those numbers.

Traditionally the chords in a family are numbered with Roman numerals. You can see this in the C major chord family shown in the following table:

I	II	III	IV	V	VI	VII
C	Dm	Em	F	G	Am	Bdim

In Roman numerology:

I = one
IV = four
V = five

Look again at the C major chord family. See the chords labelled I, IV and V?

These are the three chords we'd use in a **I-IV-V** chord progression in the key of C.

How long we play each chord for is up to us, but it might look something like this:

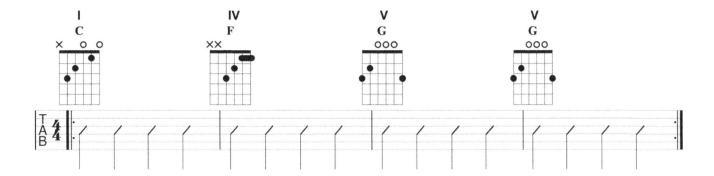

Play through this example and I'm sure you'll recognise the sound of the **I-IV-V** progression, it's used in *thousands* of well-known songs.

The 12 bar blues also uses the I, IV and V chords from a chord family. Normally these are played as dominant7 chords (C7, G7 etc).

So, a 12 bar blues in the key of C would use the chords C7 (I), F7 (IV) and G7 (V) in a specific order. Play the 12 bar blues on your guitar using the following chord chart. Optional chord shapes are shown, but you can use others if you prefer.

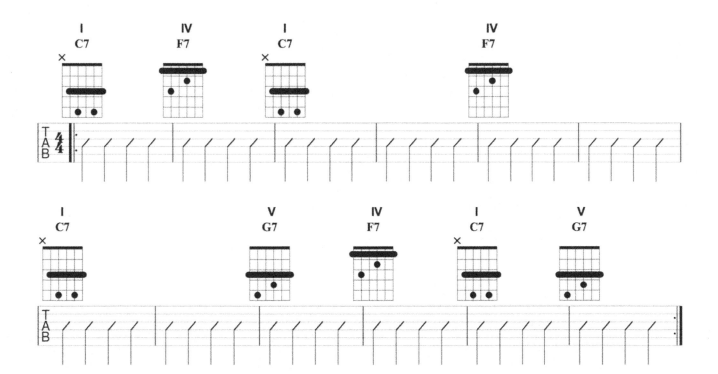

If this sounds familiar, then it's because the 12 bar blues is the basis for many famous songs, both in blues and other music styles.

The fact is, no matter what kind of music you play, the **I-IV-V** chord sequence is so common that being able to find it in *any* key is really going to help you out.

Once again, the circle of fifths makes this easy!

Finding I, IV and V Chords

Here's how you can find the I, IV and V chords in any key:

1. Start on chord I (the key you want to play in)
2. Go **back 1 step** from I to get IV
3. Go **forward 1 step** from I to get V

If we follow this formula starting on C we get: C (I), F (IV) and G (V).

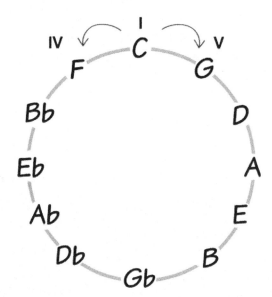

Of course, this works for any other key.

If we start on E, we get **I-IV-V** in the key of E major:

1. Start on E (I)
2. Go **back 1 step** to get A (IV)
3. Go **forward 1 step** from E to get B (V)

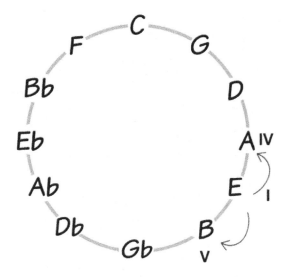

That's pretty much all there is to it, but it's a handy little trick to know!

Before you go to the next section of this lesson check your understanding with the **Quick Quiz** up next.

Quick Quiz

Use the circle of fifths to work out the I, IV and V chords for the keys given. Then fill in the blanks in the table. Make sure you *play* these chord progressions too, that way you won't just understand the theory, you'll also start to recognise the sound of them.

Key	I	IV	V
C	C		
A	A		
E	E		
G	G		
Bb	Bb		
D	D		
Eb	Eb		
F	F		

Answers:

Key	I	IV	V
C	C	F	G
A	A	D	E
E	E	A	B
G	G	C	D
Bb	Bb	Eb	F
D	D	G	A
Eb	Eb	Ab	Bb
F	F	Bb	C

Another V Chord Trick: Changing Keys

In any key, the V chord has a kind of 'magnetic pull' towards chord I. This is very useful.

This 'magnetic pull' is why we will often use chord V as a way to 'resolve' *back* to chord I. You'll be able to spot this happening in some of the example chord progressions coming later.

This 'pull' towards the I chord can be used to take us to almost any chord more smoothly. All we need to do is use the V chord of the chord we want to change to. Let's look at and play some examples.

Let's say you were playing the following chord progression:

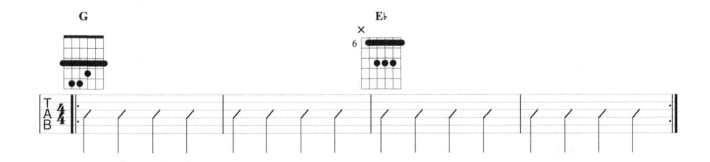

These chords don't belong in the same chord family. When the chords change, we're changing into a new key, either from G into Eb, or vice versa.

One way to 'set up' the key change better is to **use the V chord of the chord you are changing to**.

To prepare for the change to Eb we could insert Bb into the progression. This will 'pull' towards the Eb chord because Bb is the V chord of Eb.

Play it now to hear the difference it makes:

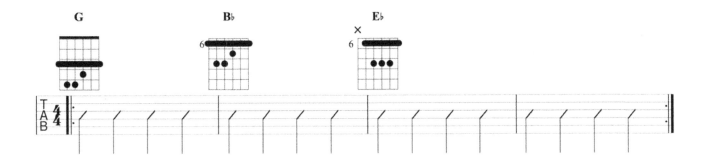

We could use this trick to take us back to G as well.

The V chord in the key of G is D. Putting a D chord in the final bar will 'pull' the progression back to G again as we repeat the chord sequence:

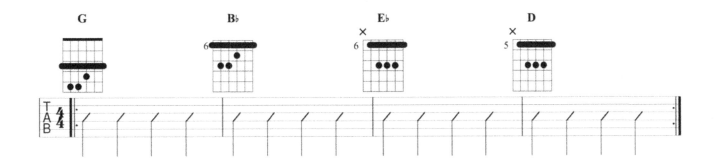

Obviously, this changes the sound of the chord progression quite a bit! This is why, as with any theoretical concept, you need to decide when is the right time to use it. Using V chords in this way is not compulsory, it's just an option you can use when you want to.

Look for this technique being used in any music you play and remember, to find chord V go **forward 1 step** in the circle of fifths from the chord you want to transition into.

That's it for this lesson, I'll see you in the next lesson to look at another super common chord sequence: the **II-V-I** progression.

Secret 7: Finding II-V-I Chord Sequences

One of the reasons the circle of fifths is so helpful for working with chords and progressions is this:

In many common chord progressions, the chords move in the *same order* that they appear in the circle of fifths

This means that once the circle of fifths becomes second nature and you can easily recite the order of the notes going in either direction, you'll be able to instantly work out the chords you need to play many common chord sequences.

We're going to see this now as we study the **II-V-I** chord sequence.

The term **II-V-I** ('two-five-one') describes what happens when the II chord in a key moves to the V chord, and then resolves to the I chord.

In the key of C it looks like this:

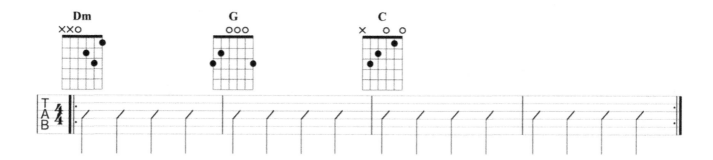

Practical exercise: play this chord sequence on your guitar to hear the sound of a **II-V-I** progression being used.

You can see this is a **II-V-I** progression by looking at the C major chord family shown in the following table:

I	II	III	IV	V	VI	VII
C	Dm	Em	F	G	Am	Bdim

Often, (but not always) a **II-V-I** chord sequence will use more colourful chords than just simple major and minor triads. The II chord may be played as a minor 7th chord, the V chord as a dominant 7th or dominant 9th chord, and the I chord as a major 7th chord.

Whichever chord variations are used, the basic idea is the same: the II chord moves to the V chord which then moves to the I chord.

Note: to keep things simpler, we're only going to play the II chord as a minor chord, the V chord as major or dominant7 and the I chord as some type of major chord. As I've already said, these are often changed to other kinds of chord, but we'll ignore that for now.

II-V-I Chords and the Circle of Fifths

Finding **II-V-I** sequences in the circle of fifths is simple:

1. Start on the I chord for the key you are in
2. Skip **forward 2 steps**. You land on the II chord
3. Go **back 1 step** from II. This puts you on the V chord
4. Go **back 1 step** to land back on the I chord

We've already said that a **II-V-I** progression in the key of C is:

| Dm | G | C | C |

We can now see why this is, by looking at the circle of fifths.

1. Start on the I chord, C
2. Skip **forward 2 steps** to find the II chord
3. Go **back 1 step** to find the V chord
4. Go **back 1 step** to land back on the I chord

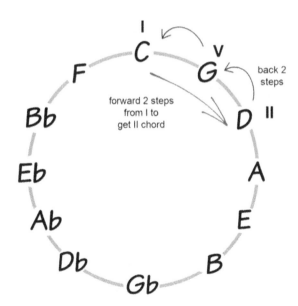

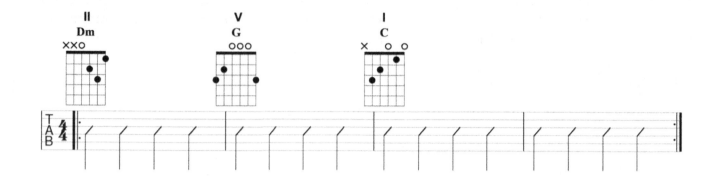

This method works *anywhere* on the circle of fifths to give the roots of the II, V and I chords in *any* key.

We can use it to work out **II-V-I** progressions in the keys of G and E♭ for example.

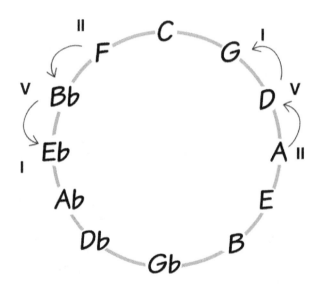

Key of G: **Am** (II), **D** (V), **G** (I)

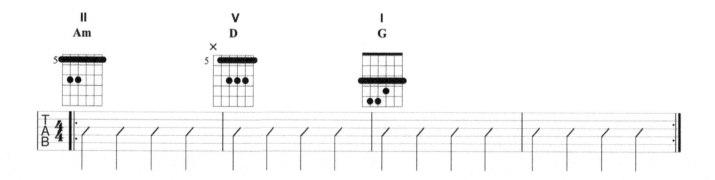

Key of Eb: **Fm** (II), **B*b*7** (V), **E*b*** (I)

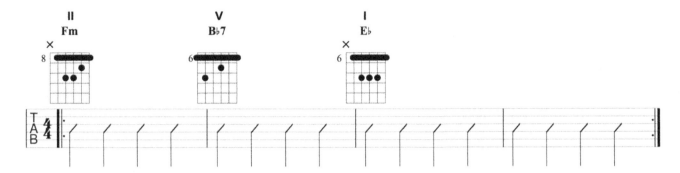

You can hopefully see how, once you know the circle of fifths, finding **II-V-I** progressions is simple!

Don't forget that in major keys, chord **II** is normally minor, chord **V** is normally major or dominant7, and chord **I** is normally played as major. Sometimes the chord qualities might be changed, but the root notes for the chords in the **II-V-I** progression will remain the same.

Don't underestimate how important the **II-V-I** chord sequence is. It's particularly crucial if you play, or want to play jazz, in this style, the **II-V-I** sequence is literally everywhere!
And that's the circle of fifths and the **II-V-I** chord progression. Before moving on, test yourself with the **Quick Quiz** up next. After that I'll see you in the next lesson for more on chord progressions.

Quick Quiz

Using the circle of fifths, work out the **II-V-I** progression in the following keys. Then **play each one** using any chord shapes you know so that you can hear the sound:

Note: Try to use the correct sharp or flat name for each chord. See answers!

1. Key of F
2. Key of A*b*
3. Key of D
4. Key of E
5. Key of G*b*

Answers: **1.** Gm, C or C7, F **2.** B*b*m, E*b* or E*b*7, A*b* **3.** Em, A or A7, D **4.** F#m, B or B7, E **5.** A*b*m, D*b* or D*b*7, G*b*

Secret 8: Finding I-VI-II-V Chord Progressions

Another chord sequence the circle of fifths helps us with is the **I-VI-II-V** chord sequence.

This is commonly heard in most styles of music.

For finding a **I-VI-II-V** progression we simply use the '**II-V-I** trick' from the last lesson with an extra step added.

Here's what to do:

1. Start on the I chord
2. Skip **forward 3 steps** to find chord VI (the relative minor, right?)
3. Skip **back 1 step** to get the II chord
4. Skip **back 1 step** to get the V chord
5. Skip **back 1 step** to land back on chord I

Here it is in the key of C shown on the circle of fifths:

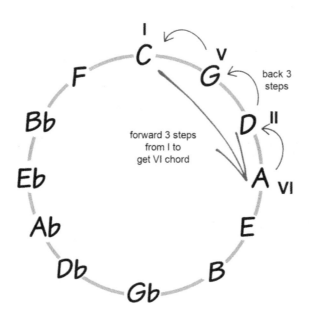

Chord VI is normally played as a minor chord.

Combined with the **II-V-I** part of the progression, this gives us the following chord sequence:

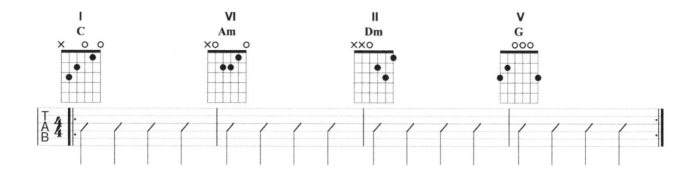

Play the progression on your guitar to hear the sound of a **I-VI-II-V** chord progression.

Let's find the **I-VI-II-V** progression in a different key: E.

1. Start on E
2. Skip **forward 3 steps** to the VI chord
3. Now skip **backwards to E** via the II and V chords

Remember to convert the flats to sharps in this key!

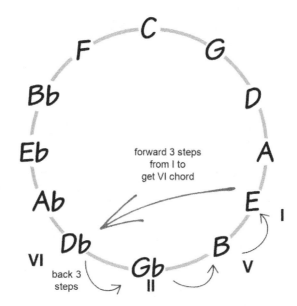

As you can see from the circle, this gives us the following progression:

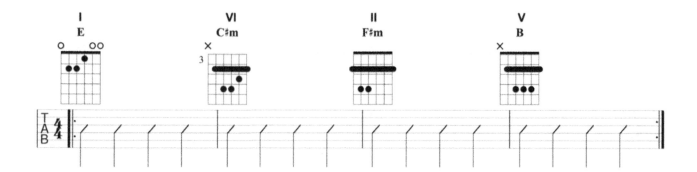

Note: the diagram above refers to D*b* and G*b* by their *sharp* names, this is the correct way to label these chords when in the key of E major.

You're hopefully starting to notice how similar many common chord sequences are. This makes them much easier to learn, remember, and be able to quickly play on your guitar when you need them.

So, that's the **I-VI-II-V** progression. We'll be seeing another common chord sequence in the next lesson. Test yourself with the **Quick Quiz** up next and head to the next lesson when you're ready.

<u>Quick Quiz</u>

Use the circle of fifths to figure out the chords for a **I-VI-II-V** progression in each of the following keys. Check your answers and be sure to *play* each one on your guitar to hear what this common chord sequence sounds like!

1. Key of G
2. Key of G*b*
3. Key of B
4. Key of F
5. Key of B*b*
6. Key of A*b*

Answers: 1. G, Em, Am, D **2.** G*b*, E*b*m, A*b*m, D*b* **3.** B, G#m, C#m, F# **4.** F, Dm, Gm, C **5.** B*b*, Gm, Cm, F **6.** A*b*, Fm, B*b*m, E*b*

Secret 9: Finding III-VI-II-V-I Chord Progressions

If we add one more step to our formula for finding **I-VI-II-V** chord sequences, we can easily find the common **III-VI-II-V-I** chord progression.

The III chord in a key lies *after* the VI chord in the circle of fifths (when going clockwise). This means we can use the following formula to work out **III-VI-II-V-I** chord progressions:

1. Start on the I chord
2. Skip **forward 4 steps** to find chord III
3. Go **back 1 step** to get the VI chord
4. Go **back 1 step** to get the II chord
5. Go **back 1 step** to get the V chord
6. Go **back 1 step** to return to chord I

Here is this formula applied to the key of C:

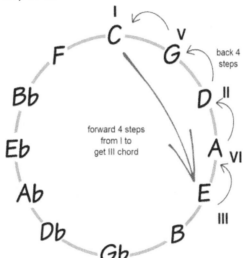

The III chord is usually played as a minor chord.

This gives us the following chord sequence in the key of C:

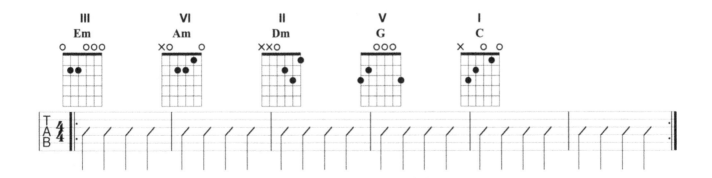

As always, *play* the progression on your guitar to relate the theory to the sound. This will help you learn to recognise common chord sequences when you hear them, a very useful skill for any musician.

Let's work out a **III-VI-II-V-I** progression in the key of B♭ now.

Start on B♭, skip **forward 4 steps** to the III chord, then work your way **back** to B♭ via the VI, II and V chords:

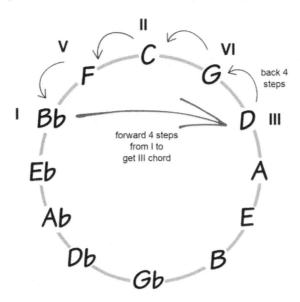

As you can see from the circle of fifths, this gives us the following progression:

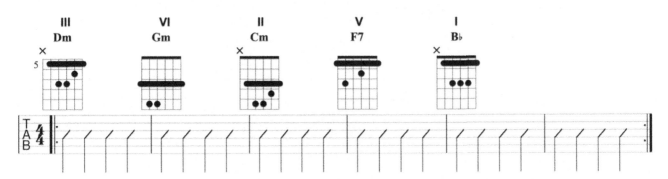

And that's the **III-VI-II-V-I** chord progression formula.

I'm sure by now you can see how useful the circle of fifths is for learning and remembering chord progressions.

In the coming lesson we're going to look at the 'master formula' for finding chord sequences. This will simplify and summarise all the chord progressions we've seen so far.

So, test yourself on the **III-VI-II-V-I** progression using the following **Quick Quiz**, then head to the next lesson.

Quick Quiz

Using the circle of fifths, figure out the chords for **a III-VI-II-V-I** progression in each of the following keys. Check your answers against those given to see how you did.

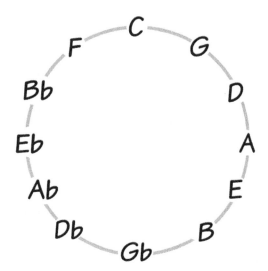

1. Key of A
2. Key of D*b*
3. Key of F
4. Key of A*b*
5. Key of G

Answers: 1. C#m, F#m, Bm, E, A   **2.** Fm, B*b*m, E*b*m, A*b*, D*b*   **3.** Am, Dm, Gm, C, F   **4.** Cm, Fm, B*b*m, E*b*, A*b*   **5.** Bm, Em, Am, D, G

Secret 10: The 'Visual Formula' for Circle of Fifth Chord Progressions

We've seen how to use the circle of fifths to work out the following chord progressions in any key:

I-IV-V
II-V-I
I-VI-II-V
III-VI-II-V-I

These sequences all use chords I to VI in the chord family, so by now you should be getting comfortable with finding chords I, II, III, IV, V and VI using the circle of fifths.

Don't worry if not all the concepts we've covered have sunk in yet. I didn't grasp them all instantly either. Just keep studying and applying them and eventually they'll become second nature.

The only chord we haven't discussed is the VII chord in the chord family, so let's do that now.

The VII Chord

The VII chord is generally the least used chord in a major key chord family, which is why we haven't paid it very much attention so far.

To complete the picture let's look at where to find it in the circle of fifths.

To find chord VII go **forward 5 steps** from the I chord. When starting on C this gives us B:

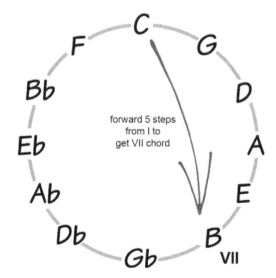

The VII chord is a **diminished** triad chord. So, in C, chord VII is **B dim**.

As I said, you'll hardly ever see chord VII being used, but at least now you know how to find it if you ever need to.

The 'Visual Formula'

We've now seen how to use the circle of fifths to find *all* of the chords in a chord family. We just need to start on the I chord and take a certain number of steps forward or back:

- Start on I and go **back 1 step** to get chord **IV**
- Start on I and go **forward 1 step** to get chord **V**
- Start on I and go **forward 2 steps** to get chord **II**
- Start on I and go **forward 3 steps** to get chord **VI**
- Start on I and go **forward 4 steps** to get chord **III**
- Start on I and go **forward 5 steps** to get chord **VII**

This visual formula is useful, it helps you see where the chords in a chord family lie in the circle. All you need to do is begin it on chord I.

Here's what it looks like in the key of C:

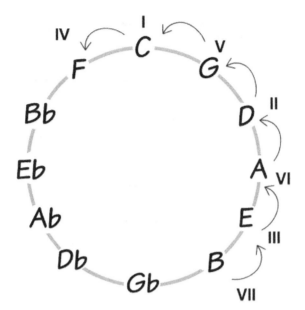

Here it is in the key of A (remember to think of those flats as sharps):

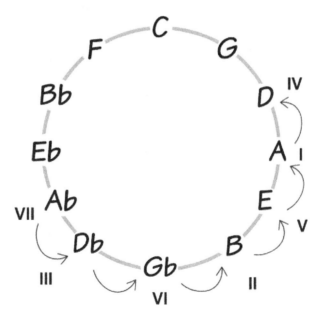

This simple formula works for every key. Although none of this is new to you, this lesson gives you a handy visual way to combine all the chord family material into one formula.

Remember, this method only gives you the chord roots, make sure you know what *quality* each chord in the family is normally played as.

60 | CIRCLE OF FIFTHS FOR GUITAR

Practical Exercise

Time to explore this idea on your own now!

Grab your guitar, choose a key, and use the circle of fifths to work out all the chords in the chord family. Then play each chord in the order that it goes around the circle of fifths. Doing this will help this visual formula to become familiar.

You can use the following **chord shapes** to play the **diminished triad** (chord VII). There are other options, but these will do for now:

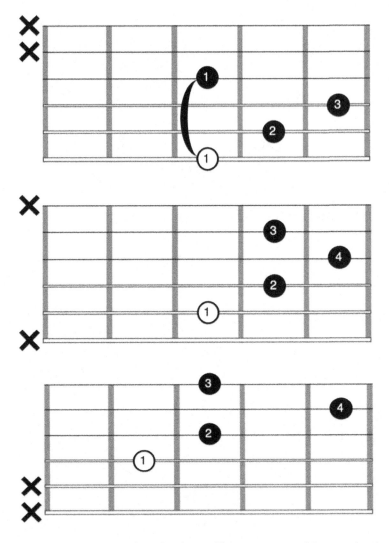

Good luck with this exercise and when you're ready we'll wrap everything up in the final chapter!

Final Words

Congratulations, you've reached the end of *Circle of Fifths for Guitar*!

You now know how to use the circle of fifths to:

1. Learn the notes on the guitar fretboard
2. Create simple but powerful practice exercises
3. Figure out the notes in any major scale
4. Work out the chords in any major or minor key chord family
5. Work out relative major and minor keys
6. Figure out how to play **I-IV-V** chord progressions
7. Figure out how to play **II-V-I** chord progressions
8. Work out **I-VI-II-V** progressions
9. Figure out **III-VI-II-V-I** chord progressions

…and more!

This is not *everything* you can do with the circle of fifths, but in my opinion, we've covered the concepts which are going to be most helpful in your journey as a musician.

Plus, the knowledge and understanding you've gained from this book puts you in a great place for learning and discovering more about the circle of fifths in the future.

I'd now suggest going back over this book and focusing on the things which are really going to help **you** the most.

Do you want to get better at writing chord sequences?

Do you need to know the notes on your fretboard better?

Is being able to solo in any key a skill you need to develop?

Decide what your goals are as a player and then use any of the relevant circle of fifth 'secrets' to help you reach them!

Whatever your goals as a guitarist, I'm sure that understanding the circle of fifths is going to be a big help, so dig in and master how to use it.

That's all from me on the circle of fifths for now, I sincerely hope that you've enjoyed learning with me. Let me know at **info@headstockbooks.com**, I love to get feedback!

If you could spare five minutes to leave a review on whichever platform you bought this book from, I'd be most grateful. It helps other guitarists see if this book is right for them, and it helps me too!

Also check out my other books and guitar products in the **Useful Resources** section at the back of this book, or visit **headstockbooks.com** to keep up to date with what's coming next.

So good luck, thank you and I'll catch you next time!

James

Free Video Masterclass

Don't forget to download the bonus resources which accompany this book, including your printable circle of fifths wall chart and the accompanying **45 minute video masterclass**.

Go to the following page on my website, enter your details, and your bonus pack will be sent to you instantly:

jamesshipwayguitar.com/circle

Appendix 1

This diagram shows you all the notes on the guitar fingerboard. This will help you as you work on some of the ideas presented in this book.

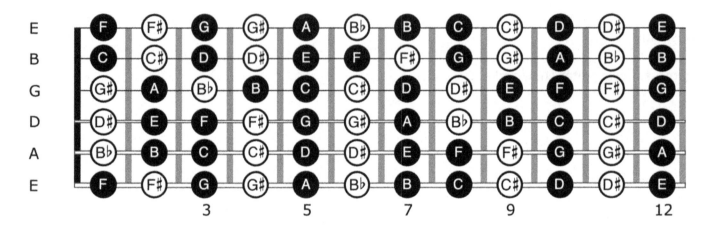

Appendix 2

The following table shows you all the triad chords in each major key chord family.

This will help you when it comes to writing and understanding chord progressions in major keys.

KEY	I	II	III	IV	V	VI	VII
C	C	Dm	Em	F	G	Am	Bdim
F	F	Gm	Am	B♭	C	Dm	Edim
B♭	B♭	Cm	Dm	E♭	F	Gm	Adim
E♭	E♭	Fm	Gm	A♭	B♭	Cm	Ddim
A♭	A♭	B♭m	Cm	D♭	E♭	Fm	Gdim
D♭	D♭	E♭m	Fm	G♭	A♭	B♭m	Cdim
G♭	G♭	A♭m	B♭m	C♭	D♭	E♭m	Fdim
B	B	C#m	D#m	E	F#	G#m	A#dim
E	E	F#m	G#m	A	B	C#m	D#dim
A	A	Bm	C#m	D	E	F#m	G#dim
D	D	Em	F#m	G	A	Bm	C#dim
G	G	Am	Bm	C	D	Em	F#dim

Appendix 3

This table shows you all the triad chords in each minor key chord family.

KEY	I	II	III	IV	V	VI	VII
A minor	Am	Bdim	C	Dm	Em	F	G
E minor	Em	F#dim	G	Am	Bm	C	D
D minor	Dm	Edim	F	Gm	Am	B*b*	C
G minor	Gm	Adim	B*b*	Cm	Dm	E*b*	F
B minor	Bm	C#dim	D	Em	F#m	G	A
C minor	Cm	Ddim	E*b*	Fm	Gm	A*b*	B*b*
F minor	Fm	Gdim	A*b*	B*b*m	Cm	Dd	E*b*
F# minor	F#m	G#dim	A	Bm	C#m	D	E
C# minor	C#m	D#dim	E	F#m	G#m	A	B
B*b* minor	B*b*m	Cdim	D*b*	E*b*m	Fm	G*b*	A*b*
E*b* minor	E*b*m	Fdim	G*b*	A*b*m	B*b*m	C*b*	D*b*
G# minor	G#m	A#dim	B	C#m	D#m	E	F#

Appendix 4

The following diagrams show you common methods for playing some of the scales mentioned in this book. These patterns are moveable. Use the root note in each diagram (shown as a white circle) to move these patterns around to whichever keys you need.

Major Scale (Root on E string)

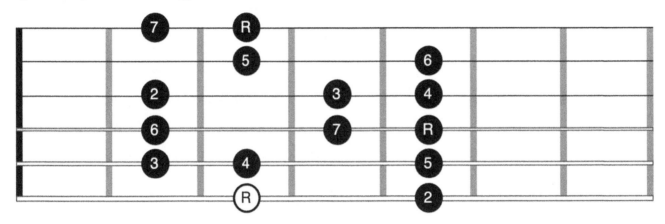

Minor Pentatonic (Root on E string played with 1st finger)

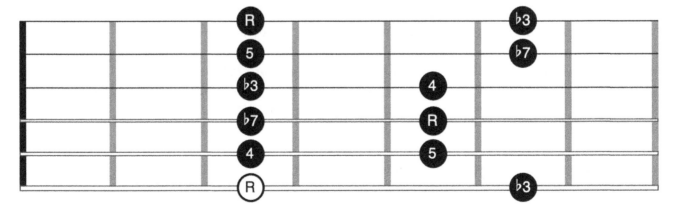

Major Pentatonic (Root on E string played with 4th finger)

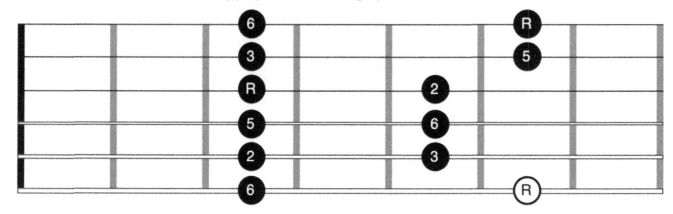

Appendix 5

The way a key signature looks corresponds to the *number of sharp or flat notes in the major scale for that key*.

For example, the G major scale contains **1 sharp** (F#), so the key signature for the key of G major uses **1 sharp** like this:

We know that the C major scale contains no sharp or flat notes. This is why the key signature for C major also contains no sharps or flats (see examples later in this appendix).

We've also seen how, each time we go one step **forward** from C around the circle, we get one more **sharp** than the major scale starting on the previous note. By extension, each time we go forward one step from C, the key signature for the note we land on contains one more sharp than the key signature for the previous note in the circle.

In the same way, each time we go one step **back** from C, we get one more **flat** than the major scale starting on the previous note.

By extension, each time we go back one step from C, the key signature for the note we land on contains one more flat note than the key signature for the previous note in the circle.

Study the following diagram. Each note is labelled according to the number of sharps/flats that are in its major scale.

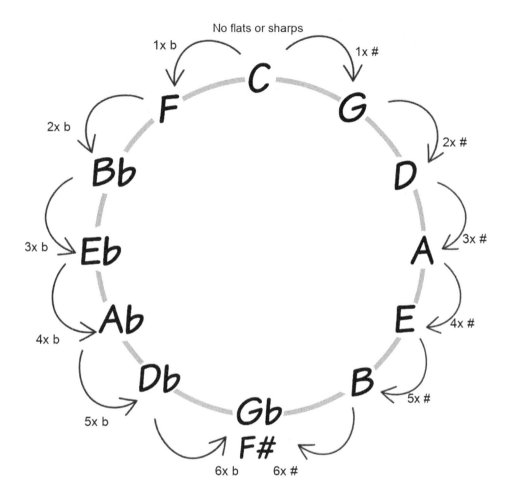

Next, study the key signatures in the following diagram to see how they correspond to this information.

The key signature for a major key is also the key signature for its relative minor key, as shown in the examples that follow.

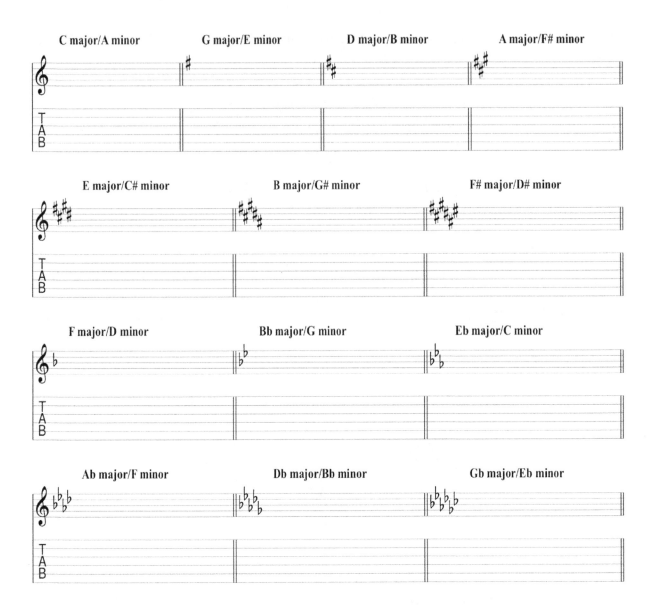

Study all this information to help this idea make sense.

You may never need to know about key signatures, but if you do, then the circle of fifths can be useful when it comes to learning and memorising them.

The Circle of Fifths

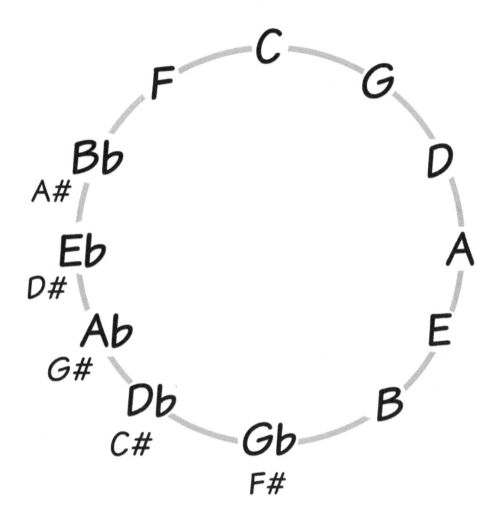

Useful Resources

Other Books by James Shipway:

Below you will find a list of my other guitar books. To find out more about each one, or to see where you can order from, please visit Headstock Books at:

headstockbooks.com

Most titles are available as paperbacks, ebooks and/or hardcovers from Amazon, Apple, Google Play, Kobo, Barnes & Noble, and by request from your local library or book shop.

'No Bull Music Theory for Guitarists'

Master the essential music theory knowledge all guitarists need to know with the original '**No Bull Music Theory for Guitarists**', the first of three books in the *Music Theory for Guitarists* series. Understand chords, keys, intervals, scales and more and become a better **musician, guitarist and songwriter**. In a few short hours this book gives you the knowledge that most guitar players take years to accumulate …and many never truly understand. **Free audiobook version included**!

'Music Theory for Guitarists, Volume 2'

Continue your journey towards music theory and guitar fretboard mastery with the second book in the *Music Theory for Guitarists* series. Discover 'sus' and 'add9' chords, compound intervals, seventh chords, key signatures, the modes of the major scale, triad chord inversions, using the circle of fifths and much more. Packed full of practical exercises and examples and **includes downloadable play-along tracks**.

'Music Theory for Guitarists, Volume 3'

Take your music theory expertise and understanding of the guitar fretboard *even* further with the third book in the *Music Theory for Guitarists* series! Learn about the CAGED System, soloing with modes, chord substitution tricks and techniques, minor key progressions and improvisation, the harmonic minor scale, extended chords, key change and modulation techniques and much more. Packed full of practical exercises and examples **including downloadable play-along tracks**.

'Blues Soloing for Guitar', Volumes 1 & 2

Volume 1: 'Blues Basics' A step-by-step introduction for learning to play blues guitar, featuring the essential techniques, scales and theory you need to know, as well as complete solos in the styles of important blues legends.

Volume 2: 'Levelling Up' This book carries on where volume 1 leaves off. It features lessons on minor blues soloing, open string soloing and scales, Texas blues style and 'jazzy' blues sounds and more.

Both books include access to a supporting website with **video lessons and audio downloads**.

'No Bull Barre Chords for Guitar'

Discover a step-by-step system for mastering the **essential barre chord shapes** that *all* guitarists and singer-songwriter guitar players need to know! You'll learn the most important and useful barre chord shapes and how to use them to play literally *hundreds* of possible chord sequences and songs. *Plus,* you'll discover powerful practice methods, exercises and 'memory hacks' to help you master barre chords without the headaches most players face. **Free downloadable play-along practice tracks** included.

'The CAGED System for Guitar'

A step-by-step method showing you how to master the guitar fretboard using the CAGED System to become a better lead player, improviser and all round guitarist.

Discover how the CAGED System works and how to use it to learn all the scales and arpeggios you need to know to become an awesome guitar player. With crystal clear explanations, practice exercises and tips, 'speed learning' techniques, as well as dozens of exciting sample licks, '**The CAGED System for Guitar**' can seriously transform your playing skills. Includes **downloadable video demonstrations and backing tracks**.

'The Guitar Practice Workbook'

The ultimate '**multi-purpose' practice workbook** for guitarists of all levels. Featuring powerful practice hacks, important scales and chord shapes as well as over 50 pages of blank tab, fretboard diagrams and chord boxes for recording your own killer licks, exercises and song ideas! Available with **free downloadable 'Goal Worksheet'** to help you track your progress and reach your guitar goals! This book comes as a paperback only.

Check Out My *Total Guitar Lab* Online School

Want to study specific guitar styles and topics with me as your guitar teacher? Well you can, with my online guitar community **Total Guitar Lab**! Join and get instant access to *all* my premium guitar courses *plus* live training, workshops and Q&A sessions. Learn more and discover the amazing results guitarists have been getting with my training. Visit **totalguitarlab.com**

Single Courses Also Available:

Some of my guitar courses come as stand-alone products. This means they are yours to keep and go through at your own pace as many times as you like.

Courses are made up of step-by-step video lessons, downloadable backing tracks, audio lessons and detailed tab workbooks complete with homework tasks and checklists to make sure you reach your goals.

The following courses are currently available. You can find them at **totalguitarlab.com** :

Blues Guitar Launchpad

The perfect course for the beginner to intermediate electric blues guitarist. Learn all the essential blues scales, how to play the 12 bar blues, authentic blues licks, string bending and vibrato techniques plus complete solo studies in the styles of blues legends like Eric Clapton, Stevie Ray Vaughan, Freddie King, Otis Rush and others! Learn more at: **totalguitarlab.com**

Minor Pentatonic Mastery

Perfect for the more experienced rock or blues player who wants to conquer the minor pentatonic scale all over the guitar neck! *Minor Pentatonic Mastery* takes you step-by-step through all the ways to play the minor pentatonic scale on the guitar. Learn all 5 'box patterns' and how to use them to play killer blues and rock licks, discover 'sliding' scale patterns, the 'Rule of 2' to use for connecting it all up and loads more powerful soloing and improvising tips to use in building an awesome pentatonic soloing vocabulary. Learn more at: **totalguitarlab.com**

Rock Guitar Lick Lab

Aimed at the intermediate rock guitar player who wants to explode their playing with the licks and techniques used by the biggest names in rock and metal guitar. Discover essential rock bending licks, repeating licks, alternate picked licks, extended blues scale licks and stretch and sequence licks and how to use them in your playing for explosive rock and metal guitar solos!

You'll also learn essential technique tips to get the licks sounding great and how to use everything in the course to easily start generating killer rock licks of your own. Learn more at: **totalguitarlab.com**

Solo Blues Jamming Workshop

Learn a step-by-step method for combining chords and licks into your very own solo blues jams! Includes play-a-long tracks, drill videos and more to help you master this fun way of playing blues guitar. Learn more at: **totalguitarlab.com**

Notebuster

Want to learn all the notes on the fretboard in the quickest and most pain free way possible? *Notebuster* will show you how! After this short mini course, you'll be able to find *any* note on *any* string ...*anywhere* on the guitar. Learn more at: **totalguitarlab.com**

Follow me on YouTube:

Search for James Shipway Guitar on YouTube and subscribe for hours of free video lessons!

Circle of Fifths for Guitar
by James Shipway

Published by Headstock Books
headstockbooks.com

Copyright © James Shipway 2021

All rights reserved. This book or parts thereof may not be reproduced in any form, stored in any retrieval system, or transmitted in any form by any means - electronic, mechanical, photocopy, recording, or otherwise - without prior written permission of the publisher, except as provided by the United Kingdom copyright law. For permission requests, contact: info@headstockbooks.com

Paperback ISBN: 978-1-914453-60-1
Hardcover ISBN: 978-1-914453-62-5 / 978-1-914453-63-2
Ebook ISBN: 978-1-914453-61-8

Made in the USA
Columbia, SC
14 December 2021